The North American Fourth Edition

Cambridge Latin Course

Unit 2

Omnibus Workbook

REVISION TEAM

Stephanie Pope, Chair
Norfolk Academy, Norfolk, Virginia

Patricia E. Bell
Centennial Collegiate and Vocational Institute, Guelph, Ontario, Canada

Stan Farrow
Formerly of the David and Mary Thomson Collegiate Institute, Scarborough, Ontario, Canada

Richard M. Popeck
Stuarts Draft High School, Stuarts Draft, Virginia

Anne Shaw
Lawrence High School and Lawrence Free State High School, Lawrence, Kansas

CAMBRIDGE
UNIVERSITY PRESS

CAMBRIDGE UNIVERSITY PRESS
Cambridge, New York, Melbourne, Madrid, Cape Town, Singapore,
São Paulo, Delhi, Dubai, Tokyo, Mexico City

Cambridge University Press
32 Avenue of the Americas, New York, NY 10013–2473, USA

www.cambridge.org
Information on this title: www.cambridge.org/9780521787413

The *Cambridge Latin Course* is an outcome of work jointly commissioned by
the Schools Council before its closure and the Cambridge School Classics Project,
and is published under the aegis of the University of Cambridge School Classics
Project and the North American Cambridge Classics Project.

First published 1970
Fourth edition 2001
13th printing 2010

Printed in the United States of America

A catalog record for this publication is available from the British Library.

ISBN 978-0-521-78741-3 Workbook

Layout by Newton Harris Design Partnership
Illustrations: Patricia Bell, Joy Mellor, Leslie Jones, Peter Kesteven, and Neil Sutton

Preface

This Workbook is designed to be used in conjunction with Unit 2 of the **Cambridge Latin Course**. A variety of exercises is provided for each Stage:

- exercises consolidating Latin vocabulary and grammar;
- language awareness exercises, mainly involving work on Latin derivations in English and other modern languages;
- exercises testing oral and/or aural comprehension;
- exercises extending and testing knowledge of Classical mythology and the socio-historical settings of Unit 2;
- focused questions on each cultural section.

The *Key to the Omnibus Workbook* can be found in the Unit 2 *Teacher's Manual* (North American Fourth Edition).

This *Omnibus Workbook* is a selection of worksheets from the North American **Cambridge Latin Course** Unit 2 *Workbook* (editors Ed Phinney and Patricia Bell) and the **Cambridge Latin Course** Book 2 *Worksheet Masters* (Cambridge School Classics Project), as well as new material created for the fourth edition.

We would like to acknowledge the generosity of the many teachers who willingly shared their ideas and worksheets with us. Of special help with the oral/aural component was Randy Thompson, Churchill High School, San Antonio, Texas, who wrote *Audīte/Dīcite*.

Lastly we should like to express our indebtedness to Fiona Kelly, our editor, for her expertise, patience, and hard work.

Patricia Bell
Stan Farrow
Stephanie Pope
Richard Popeck
Anne Shaw

Find the hidden sentence.

1   *Cross out all the verbs in the **imperfect** tense.*
   Translate the sentence that remains.

   dormiēbat Bregāns timēbātis
   dēscendēbāmus dabant dormīre
   currēbās labōrābās veniēbātis vult

2   *Cross out all the verbs in the **perfect** tense. Translate the sentence that*
   remains.

   servus intrāvērunt dedit rogāvimus in cubiculō pulsāvit
   salūtāvistī dūxērunt vīdī labōrābat ambulāvistis

3   *Cross out all the verbs in the **imperfect** or **perfect** tenses. Translate the*
   sentence that remains.

   nūllam erātis recēpit stābāmus dedimus pecūniam
   clāmābāmus petīvit vēnērunt parābās vulnerāvī habeō

4   *Cross out all the verbs in the **plural**. Translate the sentence that remains.*

   dormiēbāmus dominus īnspiciunt intrant sumus īrātus
   respondistis gladium tenēbat petīvērunt fugimus trādidistis

5   *Cross out all the verbs with endings meaning "**I**" (1st person singular).*
   Translate the sentence that remains.

   mittēbam mīsī servum habeō īnsolentissimum celeriter
   stābam videō salūtāvī possum interfēcit intrāvī

6   *Cross out all the verbs in the **present** tense. Translate the sentence that*
   remains.

   respondeō rēx audītis tibi canem ambulat
   sunt potes mittunt cantās dedit stat

The Latin We Speak

A *Fill in the blanks in each sentence with a derivative from the Latin word in parentheses.*

1 Cerberus was the _____ of the gates of Hades.   (custōs)
2 Bregans will be _____ by a nap and a snack.   (vīta)
3 The _____ of the Romans changed life in Britain.   (adveniō)
4 The solution to the algebra problem was the _____ set. (nūllus)
5 Birch, beech, and maple are _____ trees.   (dēcidō)
6 An egotist is normally not motivated by _____ reasons. (alter)
7 The school board finally decided to _____ our building. (novus)
8 The child was _____ at the holiday season.   (excitō)
9 The recipe called for _____ of vanilla.   (trahō)
10 Executing all the slaves was not a _____ option for Pompeius. (vita)

B **Antonyms.** *Match the word from the Vocabulary Checklist to the word which is most nearly the OPPOSITE in meaning. Give the meaning of both words in each pair.*

1 surgere   a nōlle
2 tācēre   b advenīre
3 velle   c dēcidere
4 discēdere   d dīcere
5 dare   e retinēre

C **Synonyms.** *Complete the following analogies with words from the Stage 13 Vocabulary Checklist.*

1 _____ : servāre :: fūr : rapere
2 contendere : festīnāre :: _____ : necāre
3 dēnārius : pecūnia :: _____ : aedificium
4 exit : discēdit :: inquit : _____
5 servāre : custōdīre :: contendere : _____
6 invenīre : āmittere :: surgere : _____

vērum aut falsum?

1 *Read the sentences below. Decide whether each statement is* **vērum** *(true) or* **falsum** *(false) and write* **V** *or* **F** *beside it.*

a) Bregāns numerāre potest. _____
b) servī labōrāre volunt. _____
c) Volūbilis cēnam optimam coquere potest. _____
d) Loquāx cantāre nōn potest. _____
e) Vārica servōs īnspicere vult. _____
f) Rūfilla in vīllā magnificā habitāre vult. _____
g) Anti-Loquāx nōn agilis est. saltāre nōn potest. _____
h) Salvius metallum novum vīsitāre vult. _____
i) Alātor Salvium interficere nōn vult. _____
j) Salvius servōs aegrōs retinēre nōn vult. _____
k) Salvius et Vārica fundum īnspicere volunt. _____
l) taurus ferōx horreum dēlēre nōn potest. _____

2 *Underline the infinitive in each of the sentences above.*

What can she, he, or it do?

In each answer, circle the correct Latin word(s).

1 *Question:* potestne versipellis fābulam
mīrābilem nārrāre?
Answer: versipellis fābulam mīrābilem
nārrāre (potest / nōn potest).

2 *Question:* potestne canis vīllam cūrāre?
Answer: canis vīllam cūrāre (potest / nōn potest).
3 *Question:* potestne Quīntus vīnum bibere?
Answer: Quīntus vīnum bibere (potest / nōn potest).
4 *Question:* potestne nauta in triclīniō nāvigāre?
Answer: nauta in triclīniō nāvigāre (potest / nōn potest).
5 *Question:* potestne fūr īnfantem parvum
tacitē ē vīllā portāre?
Answer: fūr parvum īnfantem tacitē ē vīllā
portāre (potest / nōn potest).
6 *Question:* potestne Anti-Loquāx suāviter cantāre?
Answer: Anti-Loquāx suāviter cantāre (potest / nōn potest).

6

13.5 Principal Parts

In the checklists and dictionaries, Latin verbs are written showing their main parts. Knowing them can help you to work out which part of the verb is being used in a Latin sentence. The main or principal parts are written in this order:

1st Person Present	Infinitive	1st Person Perfect
numerō	numerāre	numerāvī

1 *Listen to the English sentences your teacher will read to you. Decide which of the principal parts of the verb would be used to write the verb in Latin, and check it. The first one has been done for you:*

No one was able to wake up Bregans.

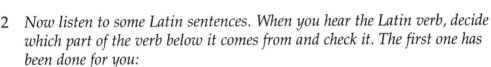

   a) excitō   excitāre ✓   excitāvī
   b) dō   dare   dedī
   c) rīdeō   rīdēre   rīsī
   d) timeō   timēre   timuī
   e) dūcō   dūcere   dūxī
   f) capiō   capere   cēpī

2 *Now listen to some Latin sentences. When you hear the Latin verb, decide which part of the verb below it comes from and check it. The first one has been done for you:*

Bregāns canem ad vīllam trāxit.

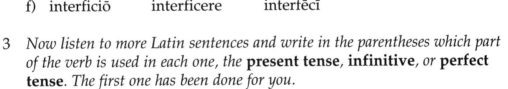

   a) trahō   trahere   trāxī ✓
   b) terreō   terrēre   terruī
   c) labōrō   labōrāre   labōrāvī
   d) īnspiciō   īnspicere   īnspexī
   e) currō   currere   cucurrī
   f) interficiō interficere   interfēcī

3 *Now listen to more Latin sentences and write in the parentheses which part of the verb is used in each one, the **present tense**, **infinitive**, or **perfect tense**. The first one has been done for you.*

Bregāns vīnum hausit.

   a) hauriō   haurīre   hausī   (perfect)
   b) dīcō   dīcere   dīxī   (   )
   c) mittō   mittere   mīsī   (   )
   d) excitō   excitāre   excitāvī (   )
   e) dormiō   dormīre   dormīvī   (   )
   f) vulnerō   vulnerāre   vulnerāvī (   )

What does he or she want to do?

Circle the Latin words in parentheses which describe the action of the character in each picture. Then translate each completed sentence into English.

1 Quīntus (pecūniam numerāre / vīnum bibere) vult.

2 Grumiō (cēnam gustāre / statuam facere) vult.

3 Cerberus (in viā dormīre / vīllam custōdīre) vult.

4 mercātor (togās vēndere / fēminās vituperāre) vult.

5 Celer (servum emere / leōnem pingere) vult.

6 servus (dormīre / labōrāre) vult.

What language did the Britons speak?

Celtic areas

Gaelic

Irish

Welsh

Old English

Cornish

When the Romans came to Britain, most of the people spoke a form of the Celtic language. Celtic went on being spoken right through the Roman occupation, and the Celtic names for places and rivers were often taken over by the Romans.

After the Romans left, the Angles and Saxons invaded England and occupied most of the country. Their language, Old English, took over from Celtic and Latin. Celtic continued to be spoken in Wales and Cornwall, where the invaders did not settle, and developed into Welsh and Cornish. Another form of Celtic was brought by the Irish to Scotland and developed into Gaelic.

FROM NOW ON, YOU'RE A HUND, NOT A CANIS.

Today old Celtic words survive mainly in place and river names. Look at this table which shows the connections of old Celtic words with Welsh, English, and Latin. See if you can fill in the blank spaces by selecting the right words from the pool below.

Celtic	Welsh	English	Latin
abona: river	afon		
lindo: lake			Lindum
deya: goddess	Dyfrdwy	Dee	
isca: water	Wysg	Exe, Exeter	
dubras: waters	dwfr		
tam: to flow	———	Thames	

Avon Lincoln Isca Abona Deva Dover llyn Dubris Tāmesis

13.8 Britannia and the British Tribes

Read pages 17–21 in your textbook and answer the following:

1 What does archaeological evidence prove about life on the island before the Roman arrival?

2 What was the Roman concept of civilization?

3 What was the Roman attitude towards the Celts and Britannia?

4 What were three things all Celtic tribes had in common?

5 What characterized Celtic art?

6 Who were in charge of Celtic religion?

7 What three things did the priests do?

8 Why would the Romans not have favored them?

The Roman Conquest

1 Who was the first Roman general to lead his troops into Britain? When did he do this?

2 How did he describe the inhabitants of Britain?

3 Why did this general go to Britain?

4 How many times did he visit Britain? Suggest why his visits did not continue.

5 What opinion did the first Roman emperors have of Britain?

6 For what two reasons might Emperor Claudius have decided to invade Britain in A.D. 43?

7 Who was Claudius' successful commander in the British campaign?

8 How do we know that his campaign was successful?

9 What happened to this commander?

10 What two things would Roman officials do from then on?

11 What were the Romans then able to do?

12 What was then the role of the Roman army?

13 Who was Britain's most famous Roman governor?

14 What did he accomplish in his seven-year stay?

Romanization

1   What was another mission of Agricola besides military victory?

2   According to a Roman historian, in what three ways did Agricola help the Britons grow accustomed to a life of peace?

3   In what two ways did Roman occupation affect British architecture and city design?

4   What was the Roman attitude to the Celtic gods?

5   In what two ways did Roman influence affect law and commerce in Britain?

6   What three things did the Roman peace and security promote in British lives?

7   For how long did the British live under Roman occupation?

Salvius

1   What was Salvius' full name?

2   Where was he born? Where did he choose to live?

3   For what did he gain a reputation?

4   In what area did Salvius first achieve recognition?

5   What did the Emperor Vespasian do for his career?

6   What religious position did Salvius gain in A.D. 78?

7   What important function did the group perform?

8   What other honor did he receive?

9   After being sent to Britain, what were four tasks Salvius may have done there?

10   Who was his wife? Where does the story imagine them living?

11   What are five pieces of evidence which tell us that Salvius and Rufilla were indeed real people?

British Farms

The first picture below shows the kind of British farm that the Romans found when they came to Britain. Many such farms continued to exist during the Roman occupation, but some British farmers rebuilt their farm buildings in the Roman style. The second picture shows the same farm after it was "Romanized." Study the pictures and answer the questions.

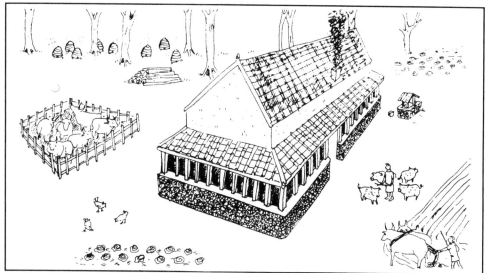

1 You are a British farmer. Why have you rebuilt your house in the Roman style?
2 What changes have you made to the building?
3 How much has your farming changed?
4 What has stayed the same?
5 What does the farm provide for you and your family?
6 What would you still need to buy which you could not produce?

Can and Could

*Listen carefully to the sentence your teacher will read to you. Decide whether the verb is in the **present** or **imperfect** tense. When you have decided, underline the **same** tense of* possum *in each sentence below. Then translate the whole sentence. The first one is done for you:*

1 *Teacher*: **Volūbilis coquēbat.**

   The verb is in the imperfect, so you underline the imperfect below.

   Volūbilis coquere (potest / poterat).
   Translation: Volubilis could cook **or** Volubilis was able to cook.

2 Philus numerāre (potest / poterat).

3 Loquāx et Anti-Loquāx amphorās portāre nōn (possunt / poterant).

4 nōs senēs labōrāre nōn (possumus / poterāmus).

5 puellae celeriter currere (possunt / poterant).

6 Rūfilla amīcās in urbe vīsitāre (potest / poterat).

7 vōs gladiātōrēs fortēs estis. vōs leōnēs necāre (potestis / poterātis).

Love me; love my dog.

Underline the correct adjective form and translate the sentence.

1 gladiātor (stultus, stultum, stultō) puellam amat.

2 iuvenis (callidus, callidum, callidō) puellam quoque amat.

3 puella (pulchra, pulchram, pulchrae) omnēs canēs cūrat.

4 iuvenis et gladiātor canem (sordidus, sordidum, sordidō) vident.

5 gladiātor (crūdēlis, crūdēlem, crūdēlī) canem (miser, miserum, miserō) pulsat.

6 iuvenis (benignus, benignum, benignō) canem (laetus, laetum, laetō) mulcet.

7 puella iuvenī (benignus, benignum, benignō) ōsculum dat.

mulcet: mulcēre *pet*

14

Opposites

Complete the sentences with adjectives from the box below which are the opposite of those in boldface.

nūllī	pūrum	crūdēlis	facile
multī	nocēns	probī	fortis
ēlegāns	urbānam	laeta	callidus

1 pavīmentum est **sordidum**. necesse est

    Marciae pavīmentum _____ facere.

2 tablīnum **inēlegāns** est, cubiculum _____ .

3 ūnus servus Salvium vulnerāvit. ūnus igitur est _____ , cēterī

    innocentēs.

4 "Volubilis," inquit Domitilla, "ego **trīstis** eram; nunc _____ sum

    quod tū cubiculum parāvistī."

5 _____ est Bregantī dormīre quod fessus est. **difficile** est eī

    dīligenter labōrāre.

6 "Phile," inquit Salvius, "tū numerāre potes quod _____ es. servī

    Britannicī **stultī** sunt."

7 **omnēs** servī Salvium timent, _____ eum amant. nam Salvius

    dominus **benignus** nōn est; _____ est.

8 Bregāns erat _____ quod canem ferōcissimum retinēbat, sed

    Salvius **ignāvus** erat.

9 Rūfilla vīllam _____ habēre vult. in vīllā **rūsticā** habitāre nōn

    vult.

10 **paucī** mercātōrēs _____ sunt, _____ **mendācēs**.

Now translate the sentences.

Singular or Plural?

In each Latin sentence, circle the Latin adjective in parentheses which matches its noun. Translate each completed sentence into English.

A **Nominative**

1 How many **cruel Romans** are there?
   est ūnus Rōmānus (crūdēlēs / crūdēlis).

2 How many **full wine-jars** are there?
   sunt novem amphorae (plēnae / plēna).

3 How many **bronze jugs** are there?
   est ūna urna (aēnea / aēneae).

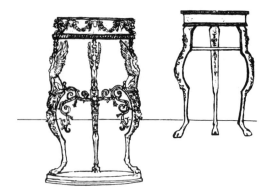

4 How many **silver tripods** are there?
   sunt duo tripodes (argenteī / argenteus).

B Accusative

1 How many **faithful slaves** is Salvius supervising?
Salvius quīnque servōs (fidēlem / fidēlēs) cūrat.

2 How many **busy slave-girls** is Rufilla supervising?
Rūfilla trēs ancillās (occupātās / occupātam) cūrat.

3 How many **big dogs** is Bregans neglecting?
Bregāns duōs canēs (magnum / magnōs) nōn cūrat.

4 How many **heavy wine-jars** are the twins holding?
geminī ūnam amphoram (gravēs / gravem) tenent.

17

14.6 Philus miser

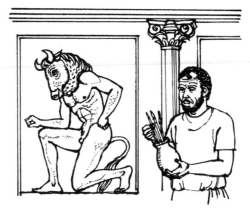

Read the following story, and then answer the questions.

Philus erat miser, quod per tōtum diem labōrābat.

"quam fessus sum!" inquit. "semper necesse est mihi numerāre. 'numerā amphorās!' inquit Vārica. 'numerā togās!' inquit Rūfilla. 'numerā servōs!' inquit Salvius. 'numerā! numerā!' semper audiō. et nunc necesse est mihi multōs dēnāriōs in tablīnō numerāre. nōnne miserrimus sum?" 5

Philus, postquam tablīnum intrāvit, pictūram vīdit. Philus pictūram īnspexit, quod pictūra nova erat. in pictūrā erat Mīnōtaurus, mōnstrum ferōcissimum.

subitō Philus pēnicillum rapuit et in Mīnōtaurō SALVIUS scrīpsit. tum, quod ibi manēre et dēnāriōs numerāre nōlēbat, ē tablīnō festīnāvit. 10

Salvius et amīcī mox tablīnum intrāvērunt. amīcī erant mercātōrēs Rōmānī. Salvius amīcīs pictūram novam dēmōnstrāvit. amīcī, ubi pictūram vīdērunt, rīsērunt.

"cūr rīdētis?" rogāvit Salvius.

"pictūra est optima," respondērunt amīcī. 15

et Salvius rīsit quod erat myops.

Mīnōtaurus   *Minotaur, a mythical monster*
pēnicillum: pēnicillus   *paintbrush*
myops   *nearsighted*

1 Why was Philus tired?
2 Why did he go into Salvius' study?
3 What did he see there?
4 What did he do then?
5 Why didn't Salvius notice what Philus had done?
6 Why do you think the Minotaur was an appropriate picture for Philus to draw?
7 Read the myth of Theseus and the Minotaur. Who were the parents of the Minotaur? Why was he half-bull? Why was he called "Mino-taur"? What and where was the Labyrinth? Who built the Labyrinth? Why do you think Philus may have felt that he was trapped in a labyrinth?
8 Research the connection between the modern antibiotic drug "penicillin" and the Latin word **pēnicillus**.

14.7 A Mountain of Prepositions

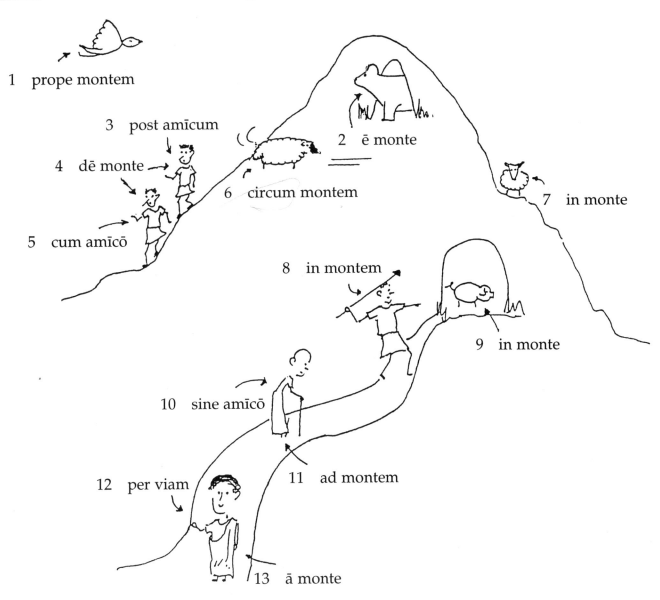

1 prope montem

3 post amīcum

2 ē monte

4 dē monte

6 circum montem

7 in monte

5 cum amīcō

8 in montem

9 in monte

10 sine amīcō

12 per viam

11 ad montem

13 ā monte

Match each Latin prepositional phrase, above, to its correct English translation.

10	without a friend	3	behind the friend
8	on the mountain	9	into the mountain
2	out of the mountain	7	in the mountain
6	around the mountain	11	towards/to the mountain
1	near the mountain	13	from/away from the mountain
12	along the road	5	with a friend
4	down from the mountain		

19

14.8 Audīte/Dīcite

*Read aloud each sentence and answer in Latin the question your partner asks about it. **A** goes first.*

New question word: **quō modō** – how?

A

1 in urbe habitāre volō.
   ubi habitāre volō? (in urbe)
2 ancillae cubiculum lavāre poterant.
   quid ancillae lavāre poterant? (cubiculum)
3 ego leōnem ferōcem vidēre poteram.
   quis vidēre poterat? (ego)
4 fūr pecūniam trādere nōlēbat.
   quid fūr agere nōlēbat? (pecūniam trādere)
5 ancilla fessa suāviter cantāre nōn poterat.
   quō modō ancilla cantāre nōn poterat? (suāviter)
6 tū ambulāre ad urbem vīs.
   quō ambulāre vīs? (ad urbem)
7 cēterī fābulam audīre volēbant.
   quī audīre volēbant? (cēterī)

B

1 in urbe habitāre volō.
   quis in urbe habitāre vult? (ego)
2 ancillae cubiculum lavāre poterant.
   quid ancillae agere poterant? (lavāre)
3 ego leōnem ferōcem vidēre poteram.
   quid vidēre poteram? (leōnem)
4 fūr pecūniam trādere nōlēbat.
   quid fūr trādere nōlēbat? (pecūniam)
5 ancilla fessa suāviter cantāre nōn poterat.
   quālis ancilla erat? (fessa)
6 tū ambulāre ad urbem vīs.
   quid agere vīs? (ambulāre)
7 cēterī fābulam audīre volēbant.
   quid cēterī audīre volēbant? (fābulam)

14.9 Word Study

A *Complete the following analogies with a word from the Stage 14 Vocabulary Checklist.*

   1 lībertus : vīlla :: rēx : _____
   2 iuvenis : senex :: _____ : īnsolēns
   3 laudāre : vituperāre :: aedificāre : _____
   4 pater : māter :: _____ : uxor
   5 parvus : magnus :: facilis : _____
   6 ad : ab :: nihil : _____

B *The following Latin phrases contain words found in this Vocabulary Checklist. Look up the meanings of each saying.*

   1 semper fidēlis
   2 Carthāgō dēlenda est.
   3 Senātus Populusque Rōmānus
   4 omne initium est difficile.
   5 nihil difficile amantī.
   6 necessitās nōn habet lēgem.
   7 Deō, Rēgī, Patriae

Life in Roman Britain

Read pages 44–48 in your textbook and answer the following:

1   Describe how the majority of the Britons lived.
2   What began to appear thirty years after the Roman invasion?
3   What were the purposes of these structures?
4   Give one sign of Roman influence on the Britons.
5   Describe the layout and building materials of this new building.
6   From what two items were the later villas constructed?
7   List thirteen things the grandest villas had.
8   What were two practical considerations an owner would look for before building a villa?

Farming

1   What were five main crops?
2   For what five purposes were a variety of farm animals kept?
3   What did ancient peoples use for sweetener?
4   Name two foods the Romans introduced to Britain.
5   How did the Britons expand their farmland into marshlands?
6   What would the occupiers of villas do to get things they could not produce?
7   Who supervised the villa? What would his standing in society probably have been?
8   What were three of his responsibilities?
9   List six industries provided by country estates.
10   What discovery indicated that there was no longer a barter economy in Britain?

The Slaves

1   What was one landowner's definition of farm slaves?
2   Compare the probable origin of Salvius' farm slaves to that of his household slaves.
3   Compare the working conditions for domestic, farm, and mine slaves.
4   Why were slaves sent to the mines?
5   In what area did most slaves continue to work?
6   In theory what protection did the law give to slaves? In practice?
7   How did the availability of slaves in the first century A.D. affect their cost?
8   What was, thus, the effect on the owner?

Boudica

Boudica, Queen of the Iceni, led British tribesmen in a fierce rebellion against the Romans. This is how a Roman historian, Dio Cassius, describes her. Use his description to fill in the details on the outline below.

The rebels considered her to be their ablest leader. She was an exceptionally intelligent woman. She was very tall, with piercing eyes and a raucous voice. A great mass of reddish hair hung down to her waist. Around her neck she wore a huge gold torque [a neck ring of twisted metal], and she wore a dress of many colors with a thick cloak over it, fastened with a brooch.

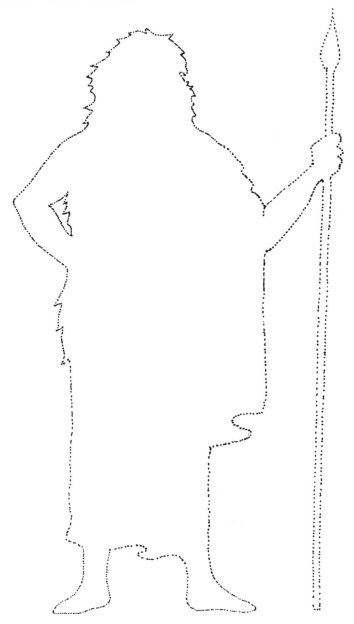

How many Britons learned Latin?

This is a difficult question to answer as little information has come down to us from Roman times. Here, however, are five pieces of evidence, some of which have been translated from Latin.

A   Tacitus, a Roman historian, writes about his father-in-law, Agricola, the governor of Britain.

   "He educated the sons of the chiefs … so that instead of hating the Latin language, they began to speak it well."

B   Writing found on an amphora in London.

   M VIIS VINI: seven and a half measures of wine.

C   Inscriptions written on tiles before they were fired. They were found at Silchester.

   a) **fēcit tubul Clēmentīnus** (**tubul** is short for **tubulum**: a box tile)
   b) **satis**
   c) **… puellam** (the tile is broken off before **puellam**)

D   Inscription on a stone coffin at York, containing a skeleton still wearing the gold ring which was worn by city councilors.

   TO THE MEMORY OF FLAVIUS BELLATOR, CITY COUNCILOR OF THE COLONIA OF EBORACUM. HE LIVED FOR 28 YEARS …

E   Gaius Valerius Amandus' vinegar lotion for runny eyes (on a stamp used to mark sticks of eye ointment).

1   *Using the evidence above make a list of the kinds of Britons who might have learned Latin and give a reason why they should do so.*

2   *How much Latin do you think each of the following would need to know?*

   a) a farmer living in the highlands of Scotland
   b) a freedman running a bakery in London
   c) villagers living near a Roman camp
   d) slaves working in the mines

15.3 Descriptions

Circle the correct description in the parentheses and the relative clause which is most accurate. Then translate the whole sentence.

1 Cogidubnus est rēx (Britannicus,
Graecus, Rōmānus),
    quī in Ītaliā habitat.
    quī Rōmānōs vexāre vult.
    quī Claudium honōrat.

2 Philus est servus (callidus, ēlegāns, stultus),
    quī abacum tenet.
    quī pictūram pingit.
    quī epistulam dictat.

3 Bregāns est (dominus, servus, coquus),
    quī semper labōrāre vult.
    quī numerāre potest.
    quī semper fessus est.

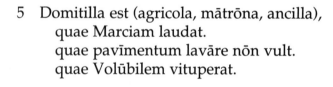

4 hic est (agnus, canis, taurus),
    quī Salvium vexāvit.
    quī Alātōrem interfēcit.
    quī Bregantem terruit.

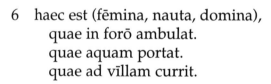

5 Domitilla est (agricola, mātrōna, ancilla),
    quae Marciam laudat.
    quae pavīmentum lavāre nōn vult.
    quae Volūbilem vituperat.

6 haec est (fēmina, nauta, domina),
    quae in forō ambulat.
    quae aquam portat.
    quae ad vīllam currit.

7 Vārica est (puer, vīlicus, arātor),
    quī Salvium vulnerāvit.
    quī fundum cūrat.
    quī cēnam optimam coquit.

8 hoc est (dōnum, aedificium, plaustrum),
    quod ūnam rotam habet.
    quod decem rotās habet.
    quod rotās frāctās habet.

24

15.4 Sailing

*The Greek word **naus** (ship) and the Latin words **nāvis** (ship) and **nauta** (sailor) give us many words in English. Write one of these to complete each of the sentences below.*

1 Several fleets of ships form a _____ .

2 A feeling of (sea) sickness is called _____ .

3 Sailors measure distances at sea in _____ miles.

4 A river which can be used by boats is described as _____ .

5 A person who decides which direction a ship should take is called a

   _____ .

6 A spaceman who sails amongst the stars is called an _____ .

7 A Russian spaceman, a "sailor of the universe," is called a

   _____ .

8 _____ engineers design airplanes.

15.5 Britain Under the Romans

Who would be more likely to make the following statements, Cogidubnus or Bregans? Put C or B in each box.

1 The Romans have enslaved many of our people.
2 The Romans have shown us how to make fine buildings and towns.
3 We now have roads reaching to the far North.
4 It is the sign of being civilized to wear the toga and speak Latin.
5 Under Roman rule life hasn't changed much for people like me; it's as hard as ever.
6 The Romans came to plunder Britain – to take our resources like lead, tin, and wool and to make a profit out of us.
7 The Romans cannot be trusted.
8 We can have the benefit of luxury goods from all over the empire.
9 The Roman armies conquer our people and live off our land.
10 The Romans offer us protection against other invaders.
11 The Romans have brought law and order to our land.
12 The Romans have killed our rightful rulers.

What is your opinion of Roman rule in Britain? Give your reasons.

The Boat Race

Read the story **lūdī fūnebrēs** *and answer the questions on the plan of the race.*
Fill in a Latin word or phrase where you see a dotted line.

Describe Dumnorix's
actions at this point
(II, lines 21–22).

_____

_____

_____

_____

Describe the situation of
the following at the end
of the race:
Dumnorix

_____

_____

_____

Cantiaci sailors

_____

_____

Belimicus

_____

_____

_____

_____

TURNING
POINT
– – – –

SMALLER ROCKS
– – – – – – – –

WAVE
– – – –

OAR
– – – – –

IN THE SEA
– – – – – –

Ship of Cantiaci:
Color _____
Commanded by

ON THE SHORE
– – – – – – –

START HERE

What three things
happen to Belimicus'
ship here (X)?
1 _____
2 _____
3 _____

Why does Dumnorix
steer to the right?

_____

_____

_____

_____

Who is in the lead to
begin with?

_____

Find the Latin for:
in front _____
behind _____

Ship of Regnenses:
Color _____
Commanded by

_____

What was Hercules' original name?

Although Hercules was also known by his Greek name Heracles, his parents had named him something entirely different at birth.

To find Hercules' original name, first fill each set of blanks with an English word which has come to us from Latin. Then write the numbered letters in the order of their numbers in the space below.

Each word is clued by a related Latin word in parentheses and an English definition.

(claudere) *bring to an end* ___ ___ ___ ___ ___ ___ ___ ___
                                                      5

(alius) *foreign* ___ ___ ___ ___ ___
                       2

(praeesse) *for the moment* ___ ___ ___ ___ ___ ___ ___
                                       7

(effigiēs) *image* ___ ___ ___ ___ ___ ___
                             4

(frāctus) *breakable* ___ ___ ___ ___ ___ ___ ___
                               1

(commodus) *lodging* ___ ___ ___ ___ ___ ___ ___ ___ ___ ___
                          3

(miser) *unhappy* ___ ___ ___ ___ ___ ___ ___ ___
                            6

Hercules' original name: ___ ___ ___ ___ ___ ___ ___
                          1   2   3   4   5   6   7

The world according to Hecataeus (c. 500 B.C.)

Look up the legends of Hercules and Ulysses. Read about the episodes in which these heroes crossed Oceanus in unusual boats.

In what kind of boat did Ulysses cross? Hercules?

A Big Exercise

A   *Use the table below to match the words in boldface with the correct form of the adjective. Then translate the complete sentence. Remember that adjectives must agree with their nouns in case, number, and gender. You may need to check the gender of some of the nouns in the Complete Vocabulary. (Unlike most adjectives in Latin, adjectives of size and quantity precede their nouns. So the form of* magnus *will come before the noun each time.)*

	singular masculine	*singular feminine*	*singular neuter*	*plural masculine*	*plural feminine*
nominative	magnus	magna	magnum	magnī	magnae
genitive	magnī	magnae	magnī	magnōrum	magnārum
dative	magnō	magnae	magnō	magnīs	magnīs
accusative	magnum	magnam	magnum	magnōs	magnās
ablative	magnō	magnā	magnō	magnīs	magnīs

a) _____ **plaustrum** viam claudit.
b) Neptūnus _____ **nāvēs** dēlet.
c) aquila ē _____ **effigiē** ēvolat.
d) ego prope _____ **urbem** habitāre volō.
e) nautae _____ **saxō** appropinquābant.
f) Quīntus _____ **tripodes** ad rēgem fert.

B   *Use the table again to complete the following phrases. The first one is done for you.*

a) magnus rēx
b) _____ certāmen
c) _____ dominī
d) _____ mercātōrī
e) _____ vir
f) _____ mīlitēs (nominative)
g) _____ leō
h) _____ ārae
i) _____ sacrificium

The Celts: Friend or Foe?

Read pages 64–67 in your textbook and answer the following:

1 What was one example of how the Romans manifested the belief that their culture was superior to that of the Celts?

2 What did the Romans leave behind after pacifying an area?

3 Under what conditions did the Romans treat the Celtic tribes tolerantly?

4 What did the Romans encourage?

Boudica and Cartimandua

1 Who were the Iceni and Prasutagus?

2 What did Prasutagus state in his will?

3 How did the local Roman administrators react to these provisions?

4 What happened to Prasutagus' family?

5 What did the Roman actions cause?

6 Name three towns that the rebels attacked.

7 Who finally won the battles?

8 What finally happened to Boudica?

9 List four facts that show some British women had equal rights with men.

10 What one right did Boudica have that no Roman woman ever enjoyed?

11 How was Cartimandua different from Boudica?

12 How did the Romans reward her?

13 What did Cartimandua do to Caratacus?

14 What eventually became of him?

Cogidubnus, King of the Regnenses

1 What was discovered in Chichester in 1723?

2 What did Cogidubnus have to do with the temple?

3 Who paid for this temple?

The Celts: Friend or Foe? (continued)

4 What tribe did Cogidubnus' family originally rule?

5 What happened to Cogidubnus and his tribe after the invasion in A.D. 43?

6 What two privileges did Cogidubnus enjoy as a possible reward from Claudius?

7 What were three aspects of Cogidubnus' new role?

8 How did that help the Romans?

9 How did Cogidubnus declare his loyalty to Rome in the Chichester temple inscription?

10 How did the inscription encourage the Britons to treat the emperor?

11 Why was that important?

12 What did the Regnenses receive besides a new king?

13 What does the palace at Fishbourne suggest about the relationship between the Romans and the Britons?

16.1 How Quintus Came to Britain

In the garden at Fishbourne, Quintus told King Cogidubnus how he came to be in Britain. His route is on this map.

1 *Unscramble the names of the countries below and put them in the correct boxes on the map.*

GTYEP TARBIIN TYLAI EGEREC

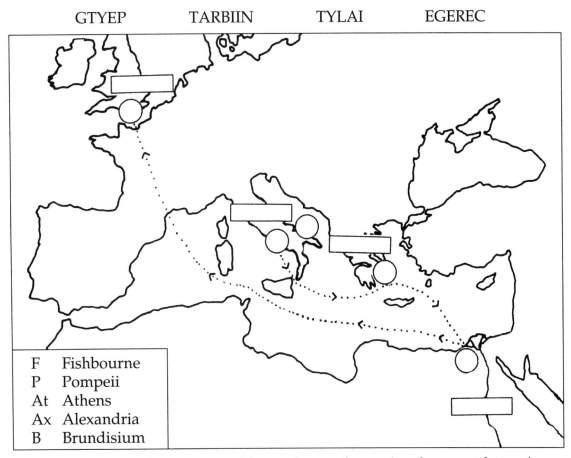

F Fishbourne
P Pompeii
At Athens
Ax Alexandria
B Brundisium

2 *Now label the five towns or cities on the map by putting the correct letters in the circles.*

3 *These sentences about Quintus' journey are in the wrong order. Read them through and number them in the right order. Then translate his account.*

[ ] et nunc, rēx Cogidubne, in Britanniā sum, in aulā tuā sedēns.

[ ] ubi mōns Vesuvius urbem Pompēiōs dēlēvit, ego et Clēmēns ex Ītaliā effūgimus.

[ ] prīmō Graeciam vīsitāvimus, sed in urbe Athēnīs manēre nōlēbāmus.

[ ] deinde ad Aegyptum nāvigāvimus, ubi urbs Alexandrīa magnum portum habet.

ACROSS
2   Roman Britain
3 and 6 across E–W defense in northern Britain
7   Number of years Agricola was governor of Britain
8   Roman York
10   Roman Lincoln
12   First Roman general to lead troops to Britain (55 B.C.)
13   Roman historian who wrote about Agricola
17   British chief who was made a king by the Romans
18 and 20 down Important Roman road: London – Wales
21   British tribe which lived in the southwest
23   Famous Roman governor of Britain
25   Roman Colchester
27   British tribe in southern Britain
28   Cogidubnus' palace may be here
29   Emperor at time of Roman invasion of Britain (A.D. 43)
30   Roman Chichester
31   Metal mined in Cornwall

DOWN
1 and 5 down Julius Caesar described the Britons as …
4   General of successful invasion of Britain (A.D. 43)
5   see 1 down
9   A British tribe in the north
11   Important line of communication: Lincoln – Exeter
14   Metal mined in Kent
15   British chief who resisted Romans in Wales
16   British queen who resisted Romans in East Anglia
19   16's tribe
20   see 18 across
22   Metal mined in Wales
24   Roman Bath
26   Roman London
29   Agricola wanted their sons to learn Latin

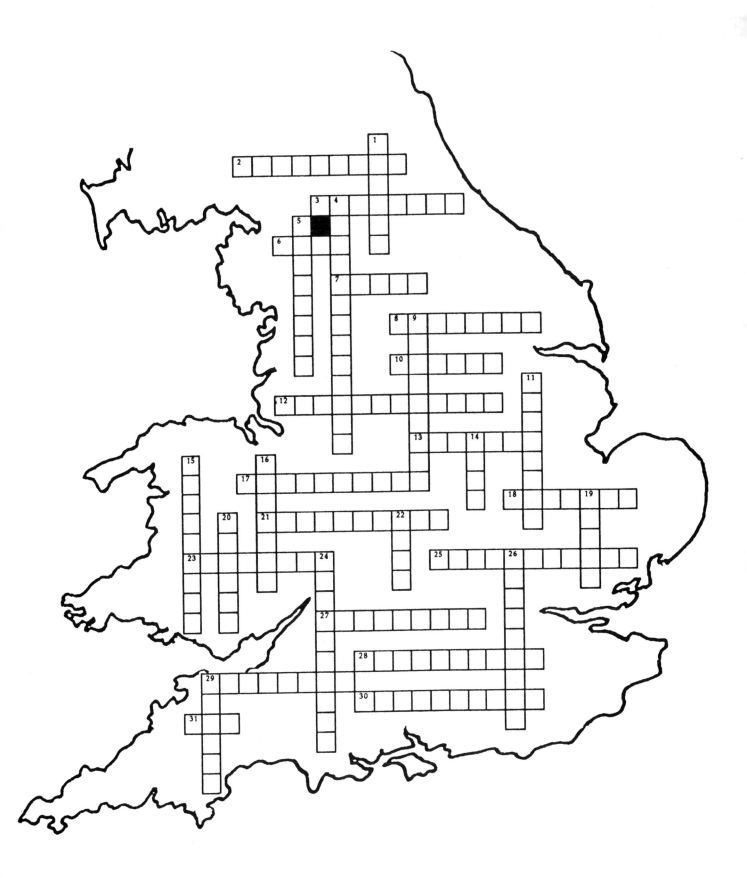

16.3 Perfects and Pluperfects

Your teacher will read out a sentence to you in Latin. Listen carefully to the tense of the verb. In the box below, check whether you think the verb is in the **perfect** *or* **pluperfect**, *then underline the correct translation. The first one is done for you.*

perfect pluperfect

☐	✓	1	Rufilla (praised, <u>had praised</u>) the slave-girls.
☐	☐	2	Cogidubnus (imported, had imported) many flowers from Italy.
☐	☐	3	Cogidubnus (led, had led) Quintus through the garden.
☐	☐	4	Belimicus (lost, had lost) his ship in the boat race.
☐	☐	5	Dumnorix, laughing, (mocked, had mocked) Belimicus.
☐	☐	6	Belimicus, in a fury, (hit, had hit) the bear.
☐	☐	7	Quintus (killed, had killed) the savage animal.

Complete the next sentences by writing in the correct translation.

☐	☐	8	Quintus and Clemens _____ from the city of Pompeii.
☐	☐	9	I _____ all my houses in Campania.
☐	☐	10	Then Quintus _____ to Egypt.

16.4 What do you see in the picture?

First study the picture and then circle the names of all the objects and persons that are pictured.

pēs	domina	pavīmentum
rēx	toga	marītus
effigiēs	faber	plaustrum
lectus	cibus	sella
equus	hospitēs	mēnsa
mūrus	ātrium	custōs
saxum	pōculum	agmen

34

16.5 Verb Building

Many Latin verbs consist of two parts, a simple verb and a prefix which adds to the meaning of the verb. For example: **con** *(together) +* **veniō** *(I come) =* **conveniō***: I come together, meet.*

You have seen the following prefixes:

ad-	to	dē-	down
re-	back, again	circum-	around
prō-	forward	con/com-	together
ē/ex-	out of	dī/dis-	differently, in different directions

1   *Attach one of these to each of the simple verbs below to match the meaning given.*

a) _____ cēdō   go forward, advance

b) _____ spectō   look around

c) _____ veniō   come to, arrive

d) _____ mittō   send in different directions

e) _____ rīdeō   laugh down on, mock

f) _____ vertō   turn back

g) _____ eō   go out, leave

h) _____ sentiō   feel the same, agree

2   *Many such verbs continue to be used in English. Using the information above, give the literal meaning of each of these English words.*

a) contain (**con** + **tineō**, from **teneō**) _____

b) report (**re** + **portō**) _____

c) dissent (**dis** + **sentiō**) _____

d) circumnavigate (**circum** + **nāvigō**) _____

e) provoke (**prō** + **vocō**) _____

f) add (**ad** + **dō**) _____

g) describe (**dē** + **scrībō**) _____

h) exclaim (**ex** + **clāmō**) _____

Relative Clauses

Complete each sentence by using a group of words from the box below. Then translate the sentences.

quod erat mēta	quī fundum nostrum incenderant
quem līberāveram	quās pictor Graecus pīnxerat
quōs in longōs ōrdinēs īnstrūxerat	quae ex ōvō appāruerat
quod rēx ex Ītaliā importāverat	

1 nāvēs ad saxum, _____,
   per undās ruērunt.

2 ancilla, _____,
   omnēs hospitēs maximē dēlectāvit.

3 mīlitēs, _____,
   interficere volēbāmus.

4 Clēmentem, _____,
   mēcum ad Graeciam dūxī.

5 Vārica servōs, _____,
   dīligenter īnspexit.

6 pictūrae, _____,
   pulcherrimae erant.

7 vīnum, _____,
   bibere volēbāmus.

16.7 Verbs with Irregular Perfects

1 *Underline the verb in parentheses which would translate the verb in italics correctly.*

  a) Cogidubnus *leads* Quintus through the palace. (dūcit, dūxit)

  b) *"Have you written* the letters for Salvius, Philus?"* (scrīpsistī, scrībis)

  c) When the king entered, the chiefs *stood up.* (surrēxērunt, surgunt)

  d) *Did you make* the bedroom attractive? (fēcistis, facitis)

  e) *We send* the slaves to the mine. (mittimus, mīsimus)

  f) Dumnorix *defeated* Belimicus in the boat race. (vincit, vīcit)

  g) *I am taking* a gift to the palace. (ferō, tulī)

  h) *Is* the king *giving* a show for his guests? (dat, dedit)

  i) *You drained* your wine cup quickly! (hausistī, haurīs)

  j) When Salvius' slaves heard about the conspiracy, *they laughed.* (rīdent, rīsērunt)

2 *Match each of the perfect verbs in the box with one of the present verbs below.*

cucurrimus	dīxistī	trāxērunt	ēgit
cōnsūmpsērunt	trādidistis	cōnspexī	cēpit

trāditis _____   dīcis _____

agit _____   cōnsūmunt _____

currimus _____   trahunt _____

capit _____   cōnspiciō _____

3 *Translate these sentences, paying special attention to the tenses of the verbs.*

  a) cibum optimum in aulā cōnsūmpsimus.

  b) ad lītus quam celerrimē cucurrī.

  c) quid dīxit Belimicus? eī nōn crēdō.

  d) cōnspexistīne plaustrum quod viam claudēbat?

Your teacher will read out a question in Latin. Listen carefully and check the correct answer.

1 a) ita vērō, servī dīligenter labōrant.
   b) minimē, servī nōn labōrant.

2 a) ita vērō, Cogidubnus senex est.
   b) minimē, Cogidubnus iuvenis est.

3 a) ita vērō, puerī amphoram portāre
     possunt.
   b) minimē, amphora gravis est.

4 a) ita vērō, equus rēgem dēlectat.
   b) minimē, equus rēgem nōn
     dēlectat.

5 a) ita vērō, Belimicus in certāmine
     erat victor.
   b) minimē, Belimicus in certāmine
     nōn erat victor.

6 a) ita vērō, sacerdōs victimam
     sacrificat.
   b) minimē, sacerdōs victimam nōn
     habet.

7 a) ita vērō, Bregāns rēgem vīsitat.
   b) minimē, Bregāns rēgem nōn
     vīsitat.

8 a) ita vērō, Salvius Britannōs
     vituperat.
   b) minimē, Salvius Britannōs laudat.

Mosaics

The mosaics that decorated the palace at Fishbourne at the end of the first century A.D. are the earliest surviving mosaics in Britain. Many of these are black and white geometric patterns that were popular in Rome and Pompeii at that time. Using the patterns below as a guide, design your own geometric mosaic. Invent some new patterns. It might be helpful to use squared or graph paper.

16.10 The Palace at Fishbourne

Read pages 83–88 in your textbook and answer the following:

1 In excavations at Fishbourne, what three things have been found that date back to the time of the Roman invasion?

2 Whose soldiers might have been there?

3 What had these soldiers accomplished?

4 What does the evidence suggest about the Romans' first two uses of the site?

5 List four improvements that were made to the area over the next thirty years.

6 What changes occurred on this site around A.D. 75 after Vespasian became emperor?

7 Why might Vespasian have ordered this work to be done?

8 List seven jobs for the Italian craftsmen in England.

9 Where was this work carried out?

10 From the remains discovered in the area of the stonemasons, how do we know that this house was very expensive to build?

11 What did the smiths contribute to the construction of this house?

The Palace Gardens

1 How were the gardens similar to the palace?

2 No matter who the owner was, what was the goal in the construction of Fishbourne palace?

3 How large were the formal gardens?

4 What could have been found growing in the bedding trenches that edged the two lawns?

5 What do the deep-set post holes suggest about the eastern side of the garden?

6 What ran through the middle of the garden?

7 What technology kept the lawn and garden watered?

8 What other elaborate features did the gardens have?

40

17.1 Where in Alexandria?

Answer the questions by choosing the correct phrase from the list below. Put its letter in the box provided and then translate the phrase. Use each phrase once.

A prope portum Alexandrīae D per viās urbis
B in cellā templī E prō templō Caesaris
C in vīllā Barbillī F in portū Alexandrīae

1 Where would you pour a libation? ☐ _____

2 Where would you see a lot of ships? ☐ _____

3 Where was Quintus staying? ☐ _____

4 Where would you find Clemens' shop? ☐ _____

5 Where would you see Roman soldiers patrolling? ☐ _____

6 Where would you find the statue of Serapis? ☐ _____

17.2 Which is the correct genitive?

Look at the first picture. Your teacher will read out two sentences, A and B. Which sentence describes the picture accurately? Put A or B in the box beside the picture. Then do the rest of the exercise in the same way.

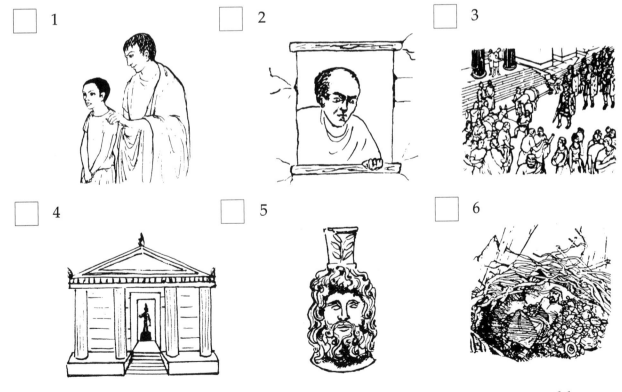

☐ 1   ☐ 2   ☐ 3

☐ 4   ☐ 5   ☐ 6

1 mercātor ōlim cum merce pretiōsā Arabiam trānsībat. multī servī cum mercātōre iter faciēbant.	2 subitō latrōnēs impetum fēcērunt. latrōnēs servōs superāvērunt et mercātōrem exanimātum relīquērunt.
3 mercātor sōlus in dēsertīs erat, sine aquā, sine servīs.	4 subitō mōnstrum terribile in caelō appāruit. mercātor exanimātus prōcubuit.
5 ubi animum recēpit, in nīdō ingentī iacēbat. in nīdō erat cumulus gemmārum.	6 mercātor post cumulum sē cēlāvit. paucās gemmās in saccō posuit.
7 ubi mōnstrum revēnit, mercātor in tergum ascendit. mōnstrum ēvolāvit.	8 mercātor, postquam nāvem vīdit, dē tergō mōnstrī dēsiluit et in undās cecidit. mercātor ita servātus est.

Linking Words

The words **tamen** *(however),* **enim** *(for), and* **igitur** *(therefore) are used to link a sentence with the one before. First read the sentences below about the Egyptian slave-boy which show you how these words are used in English.*

I used to belong to Barbillus. <u>However</u>, he gave me to his friend, Quintus; <u>for</u> Quintus had no slaves of his own. Quintus is kind to me; I am <u>therefore</u> content.

Now link these sentences together with **tamen, enim,** *or* **igitur** *and translate.*

1   ingēns pharus in portū Alexandrīae stābat. nāvēs _____ ad portum facile pervēnērunt.

2   Quīntus in vīllā Barbillī diū manēbat. Barbillus _____ saepe cum Caeciliō negōtium ēgerat.

3   Clēmēns tabernam tenēre volēbat. Quīntus _____ tabernam prope portum ēmit.

4   Barbillus Quīntō servum dedit. Quīntus _____ nūllōs servōs habēbat.

5   cīvēs Alexandrīnī erant turbulentī. Quīntus _____ nōn timēbat.

6   Quīntus exanimātus dēcidit. mox _____ animum recēpit.

7   Aegyptiī puerum necāvērunt. puer _____ Quīntum dēfendēbat.

1   *Using your knowledge of Latin, circle the correct meaning of the following phrases.*

a) A **grave** situation
   i) takes place in a cemetery;
   ii) is a serious matter;
   iii) is neither right nor wrong.

b) An **impetuous** person
   i) rushes headlong into things;
   ii) hates pets;
   iii) has no money.

c) A speaker who delivers a speech with great **animation**
   i) speaks about animals;
   ii) shows a cartoon film;
   iii) speaks in a lively and spirited way.

d) A **marina** is
   i) a lady from Mars;
   ii) a place for mooring boats;
   iii) an exotic cocktail.

e) A **facile** reply is
   i) made quickly, without thought;
   ii) full of facts;
   iii) made face-to-face.

f) An **adhesive**
   i) wipes away stains;
   ii) sticks materials together;
   iii) is an adding machine.

g) A **benign** person
   i) can speak two languages easily;
   ii) is kind and considerate;
   iii) is religious.

h) To **insulate** means
   i) to be rude to someone;
   ii) to cut off from the surroundings;
   iii) to live on an island.

2   *Now work out*

a) What is a **maritime** museum?
b) What does a **facilitator** do?
c) Why does an electrician use **insulating** tape?
d) What do people do who **adhere** to their opinions?
e) What is a **benign** tumor?
f) What is an **inanimate** object?

The Seven Wonders of the Ancient World

1 *The Pharos at Alexandria was one of the Seven Wonders of the Ancient World. Consult a reference book if necessary and then label each of the remaining six picture-boxes.*

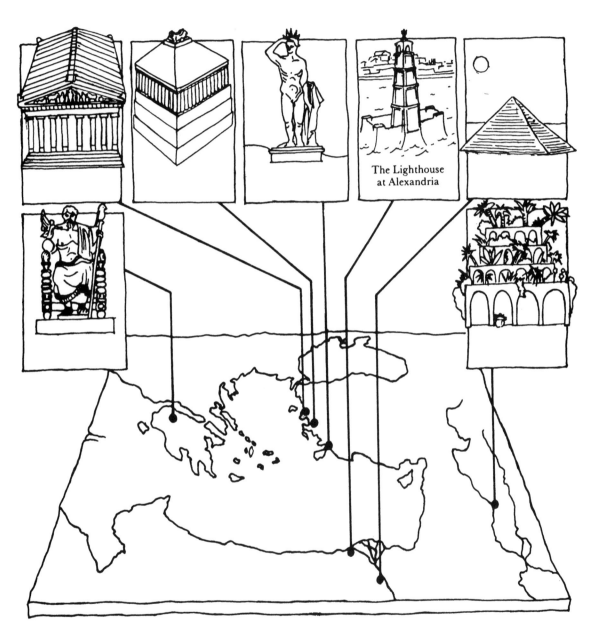

The Lighthouse at Alexandria

2 *If you were asked to name Seven Wonders of the Modern World, what would you suggest?*

solēre "to be accustomed, usually"

1 *Circle the correct form in parentheses to complete each of the sentences. Then translate, using the best-sounding English equivalent for* **solēre**.

a) multae nāvēs Rōmānae in magnum portum Alexandrīae nāvigāre
    (solēbat / solēbant).

b) pharum, quī portum custōdiēbat, cīvēs urbis cotīdiē vīsitāre
    (solēbat / solēbant).

c) ā pharō, Alexandrīnī obeliscōs, quī prō templō Caesaris erant,
    spectāre (solēbat / solēbant).

d) tum per viās ad templum Serāpidis, ubi sacerdōtēs sacrificium
    facere (solēbat / solēbant), contendērunt.

2 *Find and label, in the picture above, the pharus, the two obelisks in front of
   the Caesareum, and the Serapeum (Temple of Serapis) high on a hill.*

17.8 Alexandria

Read pages 105–109 in your textbook and answer the following:

1 Who chose the site of this famous Egyptian city and when?

2 List six things that he found in this area west of the mouth of the Nile River.

3 What was his architect told to create?

4 Did the leader see his city completed?

5 What happened to him?

6 What family ruled Alexandria next and for how long?

7 Who was the last in that line?

8 When did Egypt become a Roman province?

9 How did Alexandria compare to Rome in the first century A.D.?

10 Why was Alexandria such a successful place for trading on a large scale?

11 What four things did Alexandria offer merchants and businessmen?

12 When arriving in Alexandria from as far away as 70 miles (88 kilometers), what was the first thing one would see?

13 From what did this item receive its name?

14 What was this structure's distinction in the ancient world?

15 Describe how it guided thousands of ships to port.

16 What was the plan of the city?

17 What was the main street in Alexandria?

18 What was so amazing about it?

19 How did the main street compare to what Quintus had known in Pompeii?

20 What was the Royal Quarter?

21 What was the Caesareum? Who began its construction?

22 Whom was it first intended to honor?

23 Who eventually finished it only to dedicate it to himself?

24 Name and define the items that originally stood in front of the Caesareum.

Alexandria (continued)

25 From where did the two come?

26 Where are they now? What are they called?

27 What was another major aspect of Alexandria?

28 What was the Museum?

29 Where was it located?

30 What was so special about it?

31 What six types of subjects were researched there?

32 What did Euclid and Aristarchus produce while there?

33 What six nationalities were found in Alexandria?

34 Who were the most powerful?

35 What seven advantages did they have or enjoy?

36 What did their position cause in the city?

37 Because of this situation, what did the Emperor Claudius once have to do?

18.1   rēgīna et mōnstrum

Underline the correct form of the adjectives in the sentences below and then translate the story.

1 ōlim rēgīna (Aegyptia, Aegyptius) per Arabiam iter faciēbat.

2 in Arabiā habitābat mōnstrum (ingēns, ingentem).

3 hoc mōnstrum rēgīnam (pulchrum, pulchram) petīvit.

4 servus (parvus, parvum) mōnstrum (terribile, terribilem) fortiter oppugnāvit.

5 mōnstrum (crūdēle, crūdēlem) ad terram dēcidit (mortua, mortuum, mortuus).

6 servus (fortis, fortem, fortī) rēgīnam (perterritum, perterritam) ita servāvit.

7 rēgīna (laeta, laetam, laetae) dōnum (pretiōsum, pretiōsō) servō (fidēlis, fidēlem, fidēlī) dedit.

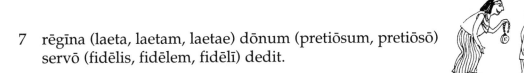

What kind of ... ?

Circle the adjectives and relative clauses which correctly answer each question.
There may be more than one correct answer in each group.

1   What kind of man was Barbillus?
    a) Barbillus erat (benignus, dīves, sacer).
    b) Barbillus erat vir,
        quī vīllam parvam habēbat.
        quem Plancus vexāvit.
        quī negōtium cum L. Caeciliō Iūcundō ēgerat.

2   What kind of city was Alexandria?
    a) Alexandrīa erat (exanimāta, magna, turbulenta).
    b) Alexandrīa erat urbs,
        quam multī mercātōrēs vīsitābant.
        quae magnum portum habēbat.
        quae in Graeciā erat.

3   What kind of man was Eutychus?
    a) Eutychus erat (probus, īnfirmus, īnfestus).
    b) Eutychus erat homō,
        quī operīs suīs fūstēs dabat.
        quem tabernāriī valdē amābant.
        quī innocentēs laedere temptābat.

4   What kind of animal was the sacred cat?
    a) fēlēs sacra erat (ēlegāns, ferōx, sollicita).
    b) fēlēs sacra erat animal,
        quod cum sacerdōtibus Īsidis habitābat.
        quod Clēmentem servāvit.
        quod caput Eutychī vulnerāvit.

5   What kind of people were the shopkeepers?
    a) tabernāriī erant (crūdēlēs, perterritī, sēcūrī).
    b) tabernāriī erant hominēs,
        quī pecūniam Eutychō libenter dabant.
        quōs Clēmēns adiuvāre solēbat.
        quī operīs Aegyptiīs fortiter resistēbant.

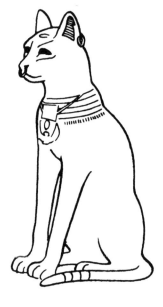

18.3 Trade and Business

Each of the Latin words in the box is connected with an English word in the list below. Match the Latin and English words. Then show what their connection is. Use a dictionary to help you if necessary. The first one is done for you.

labōrō	officīna	trādō	vitrum	pecūnia	faber
taberna	lucrum	merx	vēndō	pretium	negōtium

	English	Latin	Connection
1	tavern	taberna	tavern (an inn selling food and drink)
2	impecunious	_____	_____
3	vending machine	_____	_____
4	negotiate	_____	_____
5	tradition	_____	_____
6	fabricate	_____	_____
7	lucrative	_____	_____
8	laborious	_____	_____
9	precious	_____	_____
10	mercenary	_____	_____
11	vitreous	_____	_____
12	office	_____	_____

A Latin phrase in everyday use is **caveat emptor**. *Find out what this means. The cartoon will help you.*

Occupations

Your teacher will read out a list of Latin words. Write each Latin word under the appropriate picture on the line marked a).

1

a) _____

b) _____

2

a) _____

b) _____

3

a) _____

b) _____

4

a) _____

b) _____

5

a) _____

b) _____

6

a) _____

b) _____

7

a) _____

b) _____

8

a) _____

b) _____

9

a) _____

b) _____

You will now hear a list of occupations or trades. Write each one under the appropriate picture on the line marked b).

Glassmaking

What various methods were used to make this glassware? Look carefully at the pictures and their labels and complete the descriptions below. If your answers are correct, the letters in parentheses will make a word connected with glassmaking.

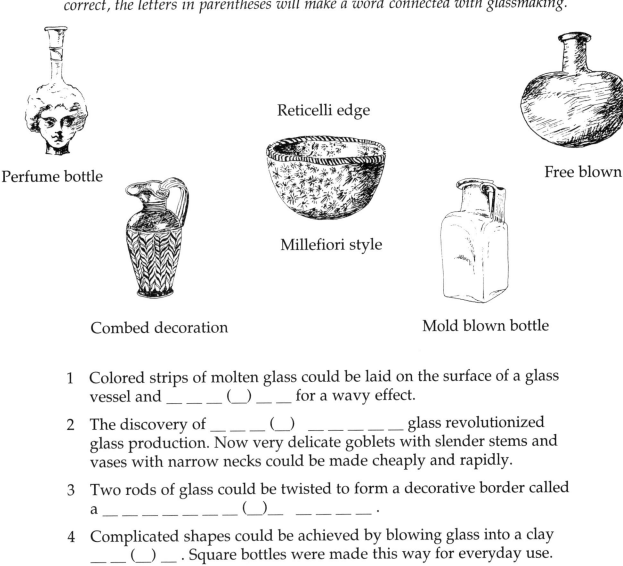

Perfume bottle

Reticelli edge

Free blown

Millefiori style

Combed decoration

Mold blown bottle

1 Colored strips of molten glass could be laid on the surface of a glass vessel and __ __ __ (__) __ __ for a wavy effect.

2 The discovery of __ __ __ (__) __ __ __ __ __ glass revolutionized glass production. Now very delicate goblets with slender stems and vases with narrow necks could be made cheaply and rapidly.

3 Two rods of glass could be twisted to form a decorative border called a __ __ __ __ __ __ __ (__)__ __ __ __ __ .

4 Complicated shapes could be achieved by blowing glass into a clay __ __ (__) __ . Square bottles were made this way for everyday use.

5 The perfume bottle is another example of __ __ __ __ __ __ (__)__ __ glass.

6 Rods of different colored glass could be gathered around a central rod and pulled thinner and thinner. This was sliced into sections that were pressed into a mold and heated until they fused into a whole. This style is called *millefiori* which means "a __ __ __ __ __ __ __ __ __ __ (__) __ __ (__)."

These were used in the workshop: __ __ __ __ __ __ __
                                           1 2 3 4 5 6 6

Quintus and Clemens in Athens

On their voyage from Italy to Egypt, Quintus and Clemens visited Greece and spent several months in Athens.

Read the story, and then, on a separate sheet of paper, write the answers to the questions that follow.

Quīntus et Clēmēns, postquam ex urbe Pompēiīs, quam mōns Vesuvius dēlēverat, effūgērunt, ad Graeciam vēnērunt et in urbe Athēnīs paulīsper habitābant. per viās urbis saepe ambulābant et multitūdinem cīvium Graecōrum et servōrum et peregrīnōrum spectāre solēbant.

forum Athēnārum quondam vīsitāvērunt, ubi multī senēs in   5
porticibus, quae forum cingēbant, ambulābant. hī senēs erant philosophī,
quī contrōversiās inter sē cotīdiē habēbant.

"est ūnus deus," inquit philosophus quīdam, "quī nōs amat."

"sunt multī deī," inquit alius, "sed nōs nōn cūrant. nōs hominēs in
terrā sīcut nūbēs in caelō errāmus."   10

Quīntus et Clēmēns, simulatque hōs philosophōs audīvērunt,
effūgērunt.

"ego et tū sumus Rōmānī," inquit Quīntus. "nōs Rōmānī nōn, sīcut
pīcae in umbrā arboris, garrīmus, sed ad ultimōs fīnēs terrae, sīcut
aquilae, ēvolāmus."   15

peregrīnōrum: peregrīnus	*foreigner, tourist*
porticibus: porticus	*colonnade, portico*
cingēbant: cingere	*surround, ring*
errāmus: errāre	*wander*
arboris: arbor	*tree*
garrīmus: garrīre	*chatter*
ultimōs: ultimus	*farthest*

1   What did Quintus and Clemens do to pass the time in Athens?
2   Whom did they see and hear in the forum?
3   How did they react?
4   Why did Quintus call the Athenians magpies? the Romans eagles?
5   Many details from the Unit 1, Stage 10 story **contrōversia** help explain Quintus' attitude in lines 13–15. List as many as possible.
6   In a handbook of Greek philosophy, research the basic teachings of the Epicureans and of the Stoics. To which of these schools of thought do you think the first speaker (line 8) belonged? The second (lines 9–10)?
7   Consult a book of Greek history or civilization, and look for pictures which will help you identify, in the picture of the Athenian forum (Greek: agora), the buildings and places listed on page 55.
    Write each letter in the appropriate box.

the acropolis:

      Erechtheum (Temple of Erechtheus) ☐

      Parthenon (Temple of Athena (Minerva)) ☐

      Propylaea (monumental entrance) ☐

the Areopagus (hill of the High Court) ☐

the agora (forum):

      Stoa (colonnade) of Attalus ☐

      Temple of Hephaestus (Vulcan or Theseus) ☐

the Sacred Way ☐

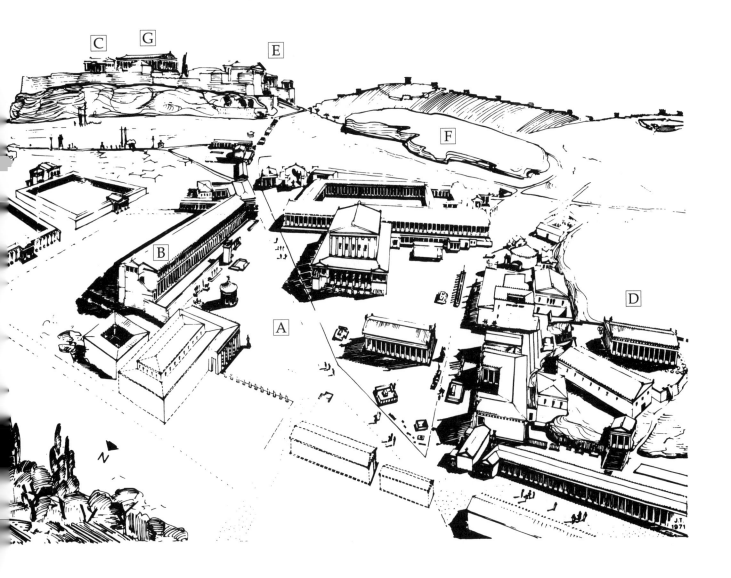

55

18.7   What's the connection?

Give the name that connects each set of words.

1   ōrnāmenta vitrea
    fēlēs sacra
    effigiēs
    sacerdōtēs
    in manūs Clēmentis
    stola pulcherrima

2   praesidium
    fūstēs
    impetus
    lucrum
    tabernae dīreptae
    auxilium

3   canistrum
    frūmentum
    sacrificium
    cella
    mīrāculum
    in capite deī

4   aedificia
    cumulus gemmārum
    negōtium agere
    lībertus mortuus
    vir benignus
    optimī situs

5   tumultus
    portus
    templa
    cīvēs turbulentī
    prope lītus
    monumenta

18.8   High Five: Odd One Out

All five declensions are represented in this exercise. Explain why one word does not fit in each set.

1   lītora   portūs   nāvēs   pōcula   undae   rēmī

2   aulam   agmen   rēgem   metallum   caerimōniam   imperium

3   faciēs   pedēs   impetūs   umerōs   manūs   capillōs

4   ōrnāmenta   cubicula   mīrācula   āra   ōscula   sacrificia

5   faciēī   agminis   lucrī   impetūs   praemia   situs

6   manūs   faciēs   caput   nox   pars   dea

7   aliquid   certāmen   lītus   portus   signum   vitreum

18.9 Glassmaking

Read pages 127–130 in your textbook and answer the following:

1 What was one of the oldest and most successful industries in Alexandria?

2 What is the date of the earliest known Egyptian glass?

3 What is glass made from?

4 What was its earliest use?

5 Describe the first method for shaping heated glass.

6 What was the only suitable use for this type of glass?

7 Name and describe the second glassmaking technique.

8 What are two impressive specimens of glass created by this technique?

9 Describe how millefiori and ribbon glass were produced.

10 List four drawbacks to all glass produced by this second glassmaking technique.

11 What discovery in the first century B.C. produced a revolution in glassmaking?

12 Describe the free-blowing technique.

13 Where might we see this technique used today?

14 How does mold-blowing differ from free-blowing?

15 What three advantages made this first-century B.C. invention almost completely replace the second glassmaking technique?

16 What were the results of this invention on the glass market place?

17 What is the color of natural glass?

18 What is the reason for colors in glass?

19 When glassmakers learned to create clear glass, what property did they discover about glass?

20 How did this discovery affect the popularity of clear and colored glass?

21 As the production of glass spread throughout the ancient world, what was becoming more common?

22 What five characteristics made glass containers reusable?

23 Once the Romans discovered that windows could be made from glass, what buildings, in particular, profited from its use?

24 Which glass industry finally equaled or surpassed the skill of ancient glassmakers?

18.10 Egypt

Read pages 131–134 in your textbook and answer the following:

1 What were two effects of the annual flooding of the Nile?

2 What did these effects then produce?

3 Who were the first three ruling groups of Egypt before the arrival of the Romans?

4 Describe the system these rulers set up to get as much as possible out of the land for their own advantage.

5 Describe the peasants' lives.

6 To what extent did the arrival of the Romans change the lives of the peasants?

7 What was Rome's major concern?

8 Why was it so important for the Romans to ensure that things stayed the same in Egypt?

9 Given the unchanging situation and the special breaks given to Greeks and Romans, what were three not unexpected results commonly seen in the society?

10 List five items commonly imported to Rome from Egypt.

11 Which three Egyptian gods were widely worshiped throughout the Roman world?

12 How did some Roman emperors imitate Egyptian pharaohs?

13 Describe how the Romans melded their taste for highly individualized portraiture with the Egyptian funerary practice of mummification.

19.1 Genitive Singular or Plural

Complete the sentences below by choosing one of the genitives from the parentheses. The pictures tell you whether the genitive singular or plural is required. Then translate the whole sentence.

1 Helena est amīca _____ .
   (iuvenis, iuvenum)

2 rosae _____ sunt pulchrae.
   (puellae, puellārum)

3 canēs _____ sunt parvī.
   (puerī, puerōrum)

4 nōs dentēs _____ timēmus.
   (leōnis, leōnum)

5 sanguis _____ valdē fluēbat.
   (mōnstrī, mōnstrōrum)

6 Aristō est scrīptor _____ .
   (tragoediae, tragoediārum)

7 latrōnēs mercem _____ rapuērunt.
   (mercātōris, mercātōrum)

This activity is based on the stories **pompa** *and* **nāvis sacra.**
Using the following selected sentences draw the procession of Isis and decorate the ship. Label your pictures with the correct letter. The front of the procession should be near the harbor.

pompa

A   puellae flōrēs spectātōribus dabant et in viam spargēbant.

B   puerī carmina dulcia cantābant.

C   tubicinēs tubās īnflābant.

D   quattuor sacerdōtēs effigiem deae in umerīs ferēbant.

E   stola deae crocea et pulcherrima erat.

in portū

F   multī cīvēs rosās in nāvem et in mare iaciēbant.

G   puppis nāvis erat aurāta.

H   corōna rosārum dē mālō nāvis pendēbat.

60

hic haec hoc

To complete the sentences put in the correct word from the table. Then translate your sentences.

	singular			plural		
	masculine	feminine	neuter	masculine	feminine	neuter
nominative	hic	haec	hoc	hī	hae	haec
accusative	hunc	hanc	hoc	hōs	hās	haec

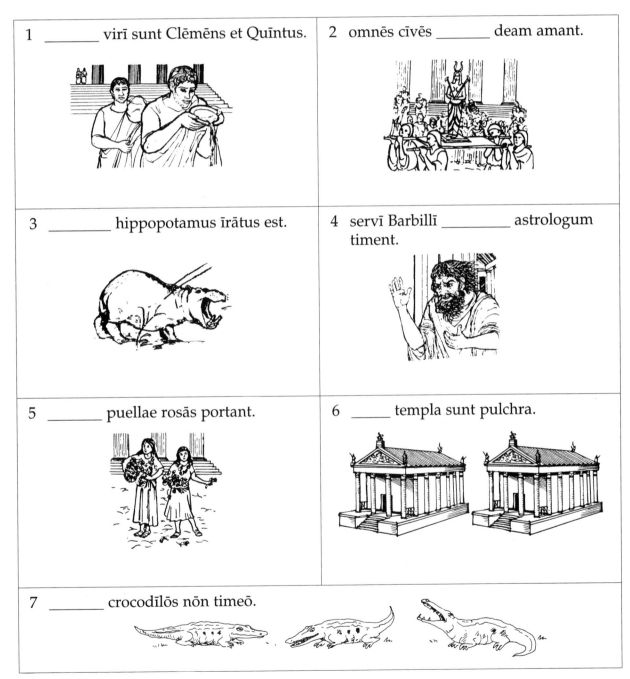

1 _____ virī sunt Clēmēns et Quīntus.

2 omnēs cīvēs _____ deam amant.

3 _____ hippopotamus īrātus est.

4 servī Barbillī _____ astrologum timent.

5 _____ puellae rosās portant.

6 _____ templa sunt pulchra.

7 _____ crocodīlōs nōn timeō.

Signs of the Zodiac

The astrologer who lived in Barbillus' house believed that predictions could be made about the life of a person according to the exact date and hour of his or her birth. The twelve constellations of the zodiac encircle the earth and the sun appears to travel through them in the course of a year.

Fill in the missing Latin and English names on the chart, and then answer the questions which follow.

Aquarius	The _____ carrier
Pisces	The _____
Aries	The _____
_____	The bull
_____	The twins
Cancer	The _____
_____	The lion
Virgo	The _____
Libra	The _____
Scorpio	The _____
Sagittarius	The archer
Capricornus	The goat

1   Zodiac means "living creatures." Which sign is the odd one out?

2   From which Latin words do the English words in boldface come? What do they mean?

	Latin	English
a) the **solar** system	_____	_____
b) the **constellation** of Leo	_____	_____
c) the **celestial** sphere	_____	_____
d) the **lunar** calendar	_____	_____

3   In Greek mythology, who were the centaur and the twins who gave their names to Sagittarius and Gemini?

62

Improve your imperatives!

Choose the appropriate word in parentheses and complete the sentences. Then translate the sentences.

1. Aristō poētae, quī versūs scurrīlēs recitābat, exclāmāvit:
   " _____ !" (abī, abīte)

2. in portū Alexandrīae Helena clāmāvit:
   "māter! pater! _____ nāvem!" (spectā, spectāte)

3. Galatēa fīliam vocāvit.
   " _____ prope mē!" inquit. (stā, stāte)

4. ubi iuvenēs Helenam avidī spectābant, māter clāmāvit:
   " _____ nōs vexāre!" (nōlī, nōlīte)

5. astrologus Barbillum monuit:
   " _____ hodiē ē vīllā exīre!" (nōlī, nōlīte)

6. Phormiō servōs iussit:
   "hastās ad flūmen _____ !" (portā, portāte)

7. Barbillus, postquam hastam Quīntō dedit, dīxit:
   " _____ crocodīlum!" (necā, necāte)

8. Barbillus, ubi in aquam dēcidit, servīs clāmāvit:
   "mē _____ !" (servā, servāte)

vērum aut falsum?

*Your teacher will read four sentences about each picture. Decide whether each statement is **vērum** or **falsum** and write the answers (**V** or **F**) underneath each picture.*

A

1 ___
2 ___
3 ___
4 ___

B

1 ___
2 ___
3 ___
4 ___

C

1 ___
2 ___
3 ___
4 ___

D

1 ___
2 ___
3 ___
4 ___

fēminae Alexandrīnae

Translate the following story.

Praxinoa cum īnfante suō amīcam exspectat. amīca est Gorgō. ancilla, Eunoa, quoque adest. mox Gorgō advenit.

Gorgō: tūne ades, Praxinoa?

Praxinoa: Gorgō! ecce! adsum. exspectātissima es. Eunoa! fer sellam! impōne pulvīnum!

G: benigna es. quam pulcher pulvīnus!

P: sedē!

G: quam fessa sum! vix tūta hūc advēnī. tanta erat turba, tot equitēs. iter sine fīne erat. procul ab urbe habitās, mea Praxinoa.

P: marītus meus est asinus. ad fīnem Aegyptī mē trahit. ibi casam ēmit, nōn vīllam! nōbīs invidet, quod amīcae sumus. quam stultus est marītus meus!

G: nōlī marītum vituperāre, mea cārissima! ecce! (*ad īnfantem sē vertit.*) īnfāns tē spectat. nōlī sollicitus esse, Kyrille! nōs nōn dē patre tuō dīcimus.

P: ō mē miseram! īnfāns rem intellegit.

G: optimus est pater tuus, Kyrille!

P: heri ego patrī dīxī, "fer mihi pānem ā tabernā!" ille tamen caudex mihi carnem tulit.

G: marītus meus stultissimus quoque est. pecūniam floccī nōn facit. heri quīnque tunicās sibi ēmit, quae sordidissimae erant. sed septem dēnāriōs trādidit. ēheu! sed indue pallam tuam! necesse est nōbīs exīre. est enim hodiē in urbe pompa magnifica.

P: optimē! ego quoque hanc pompam spectāre volō.

G: tum posteā cum amīcīs nostrīs dē eā garrīre possumus. venī! esne parāta?

P: Eunoa! cape hanc lānam! impōne in armārium! nam fēlēs in lānā semper dormīre vult. Eunoa! festīnā! fer mihi aquam statim! faciem lavāre volō. (*īnfāns lacrimat.*) minimē, Kyrille, tū nōbīscum venīre nōn potes. nōlī lacrimāre, meum mel. dā mihi ōsculum! (*Eunoa aquam fert.*) funde aquam! cavē, īnsāna! tū stolam meam madidam facis!

G: satis pulchra es! nōs festīnāre dēbēmus. (*exeunt.*)

fer: ferre	*bring*	carnem: carō	*meat*
impōne: impōnere	*put on, put into*	indue: induere	*put on*
pulvīnum: pulvīnus	*cushion*	pallam: palla	*cloak*
fīne: fīnis	*end*	lānam: lāna	*wool*
nōbis invidet	*is jealous of us*	faciem: faciēs	*face*
pānem: pānis	*bread*	cavē: cavēre	*beware*

19.8 Io, the Human Cow

Read the story below, and then write the answers to the questions that follow.

Īō, vacca hūmānā

Io was a Greek nymph who attracted the attention of Jupiter, king of the gods. Because his wife Juno was jealous, Jupiter tried to protect Io by turning her into a cow.

Iuppiter Īō, nympham pulcherrimam, in figūram vaccae niveae vertit. Īō
īnfēlīx igitur aliquandō, in terrā recumbēns, grāmen frūmentumque
dūrum cōnsūmēbat, aliquandō, vix ē terrā surgēns, aquam ē flūmine
sordidō bibēbat.

    Īō vacca, ubi manūs pedēsque īnspicere temptāvit, ungulās nigrās   5
vīdit. Īō vacca, ubi stolam nitidam īnspicere temptāvit, villōs niveōs vīdit.
"ō mē miseram!" sēcum cōgitābat; ubi tamen "ō mē miseram!" dīcere
temptāvit, cum magnō gemitū mū ... mūgīvit.

    ōlim Īō, postquam patrem Īnachum forte cōnspexit, Īnachō
appropinquāvit et eī ōsculum dare temptāvit.   10

    "babae! quid agis, vacca?" exclāmāvit pater. "tū es animal valdē
molestum! abī, coniunge tē cum cēterīs vaccīs, quae in agrō sunt!"

    subitō Īō trīstissimē mūgīvit et, postquam crūs dextrum sustulit et
lentē dēmīsit, ungulam in pulverem firmē impressit et lentē scrībere
coepit: 15

I

et deinde difficulter cōnfēcit:
O

    "ō mē miserum!" lacrimāvit pater. "tū es Īō, fīlia mea, et, quamquam
in corpore vaccae habitās, mihi cārissima es."   20

But Io's reunion with her father was brief. Jealous Juno sent a gadfly which kept buzzing and biting Io, slowly driving her away from Greece, across land and sea, to Egypt. There, by the banks of the Nile, Io sank down weary, and Jupiter, out of pity, restored her to human shape. The local Egyptians, because they mistook Io for Isis, worshiped her like a goddess.

Io: Io	*Io (Greek nom. & acc.)*	Īnachum: Īnachus	*Inachus (King of Argos)*
figūram: figūra	*shape*	crūs: crūs	*leg*
aliquandō	*sometimes*	dēmīsit: dēmittere	*lower, let down*
grāmen: gramen	*grass*	pulverem: pulvis	*dust*
ungulās: ungula	*hoof*	difficulter	*with difficulty*
villōs: villī	*shaggy hairs*	corpore: corpus	*body*
mūgīvit: mūgīre	*moo*		

66

1 How did the cow Io pass her time?
2 What did she see when she tried to look at her hands and feet? at her gleaming dress?
3 What happened when she tried to complain?
4 What did she do when she caught sight of her father?
5 How did her father react at first?
6 What did Io do then?
7 How did her father react this second time?
8 Why do you think the Egyptians mistook Io for Isis?

19.9 | What do you see in the picture?

First study the picture below and then circle what you see.

If you wish, study again the plan of a Pompeian house in Unit 1, Stage 1, page 13. Barbillus' Roman-style house in Alexandria would not have been appreciably different from an elegant house in Pompeii.

peristȳlium   tunica
valvae   culīna
latrīna   pavīmentum
hortus   fēlēs
aqua   impluvium
mūrī   larārium
candēlābrum   tablīnum
toga   armārium
triclīnium   columnae
stola   statuae
ānulus   ātrium
mēnsa   sella

Who is this? Who are these?

Circle the correct Latin word in parentheses, and then translate the sentences. You may need to consult the Complete Vocabulary for gender.

1 a) (haec / hoc / hic) vir est Aristō, quī tragoediās
scrībere vult.
  b) amīcī (hoc / hanc / hunc) virum numquam
vīsitant, quod semper tragoediās recitat.

2 a) (hoc / haec / hic) fēmina est Galatēa, uxor
Aristōnis.
  b) tībīcinēs et citharoedī (hoc / hunc / hanc)
fēminam semper vīsitant, quod cantāre et iocōs
facere vult.

3 a) (hī / hae) puellae corōnās rosārum gerunt.
  b) tubicinēs post (hās / hōs) puellās prōcēdunt.

4 a) (hic / haec / hoc) sacerdōs deae Īsidī
sacrificium facit.
  b) multī aliī hominēs (hoc / hanc / hunc)
sacerdōtem spectant et versūs sacrōs recitant.

5 a) (hic / hoc / haec) animal est Ariēs.
  b) vīdistīne (hanc / hunc / hoc) animal? in terrā
nōn habitat.

6 a) (hī / hae) crocodīlī in aquam ruunt.
  b) vēnātōrēs (hās / hōs) crocodīlōs interficere
volunt.

Word Study

A *Give an English word from the Latin word in parentheses to complete each sentence.*

  1 There was a great ____ of refugees from the hurricane. (fluere)
  2 The recipe called for ____ sugar. (cōnficere)
  3 We will always ____ these memories. (cārus)
  4 The tenor's ____ tones resounded throughout the music hall. (dulcis)
  5 The chairman refused to ____ funds to our committee. (locus)

B *Match the word from the Stage 19 Vocabulary Checklist to its antonym. Give the meaning of both words in each pair.*

  1 raucus   a illūc
  2 paucissimī   b plūrimī
  3 nocte   c sonitus
  4 laudāre   d māne
  5 fīlius   e cōnfēcī
  6 vituperāre   f dulcis
  7 silentium   g grātiās agere
  8 hūc   h castigāre
  9 coepī   i fīlia

C *Look up the meaning of these famous Latin sayings which contain words from the Stage 19 Vocabulary Checklist. Where possible, find the authors of the saying. Which sayings do you agree with? disagree with? Explain your answers.*

  1 cōgitō, ergō sum.
  2 medice, cūrā tē ipsum.
  3 sī vīs amārī, amā!
  4 dulce et decōrum est prō patriā morī.
  5 audī, vidē, tacē, sī vīs vīvere in pāce.
  6 amantēs sunt āmentēs.
  7 vōx populī, vōx deī.
  8 vīxēre fortēs ante Agamemnona. [vīxēre=vīxērunt]
  9 quī mē amat, amat et canem meam.
  10 quī bene amat, bene castīgat.

The Worship of Isis

Read pages 154–158 in your textbook and answer the following:

1 How did Isis rank among the Egyptian hierarchy of gods?

2 For what two aspects did the Egyptians worship Isis?

3 What was the status of women in the cult of Isis?

4 When was Isis' most important festival?

5 What season did it mark?

6 Why was that season so important to the Romans?

7 Describe the procession to the Great Harbor.

8 What was a **sistrum**?

9 Describe the boat in the harbor and its fate.

10 What happened to the statue after the harbor ceremony?

11 What is a **cella**?

12 What were two different aspects of this religious ceremony?

13 Who were the **Īsiacī**?

14 What did one have to do to become an **Īsiacus**?

15 Why is *The Golden Ass* important for our study of Isis?

16 What were five things a person had to do to be prepared for membership in the brotherhood?

17 How well known were the initiation rites in the outside community?

18 What two things did new initiates believe had happened or would happen to them?

19 How widespread was the cult of Isis?

20 What had happened to her priests in Pompeii?

20.1 Who's Who in Alexandria

Your teacher will ask you a question. Circle the correct answer a), b), *or* c).

1 a)    b)    c)

2 a) Galatēa   b) Plōtīna   c) Helena
3 a) Clēmēns   b) mercātor Arabs   c) Barbillus
4 a) crocodīlī   b) leōnēs   c) ursae

5 a)    b)    c)

6 a) servī   b) mīlitēs   c) mercātōrēs
7 a) Quīntus   b) Barbillus   c) Aristō
8 a) Phormiō   b) Clēmēns   c) Petrō

9 a)    b)    c)

10 a) Galatēa   b) Plōtīna   c) Helena
11 a) Plancus   b) Eutychus   c) Clēmēns
12 a) Eutychus   b) fēlēs sacra   c) Rūfus

Papyrus

Papyrus was used throughout the Roman world as a writing material. The best examples come from the garbage dumps and tombs of Roman Egypt where the dry sands have helped to preserve them. All sorts of writing in Latin and Greek have been discovered, from plays and poetry to legal documents and private letters.

The imitation papyrus below tells you how papyrus was made and used. The writing is set out as on ancient papyrus, with no spacing or punctuation. Write out what it says, making guesses where parts are missing.

CMS = centimeters

The long strip of papyrus was rolled up into a scroll. This was known as a **volūmen** *(from the Latin word* **volvere**, *which means "to roll").*

Its ends were smoothed off with pumice and dyed black. A rod of wood or ivory, known as an **umbilīcus**, *was attached to each end of the scroll. You read the* **volūmen** *by unrolling it with your right hand and rolling it up with your left. The* **umbilīcus** *had ornamental knobs, sometimes in the shape of horns (hence their name:* **cornua**). *The title of the book (* **titulus**) *was written on a strip of parchment and attached to the scroll. The scrolls would then be laid on a shelf or stored in a cylindrical box known as a* **capsa**.

You wrote on papyrus with a reed or goose quill (**penna**); *you used ink made from soot and resin, diluted as necessary.*

Whenever a Roman talked of "books" (**librī**), *he meant papyrus scrolls.*

Now label the drawings with the correct Latin words in the spaces marked L. Then write an English word derived from the Latin in the space labeled E. One of them has been done for you. You may need a dictionary to help you.

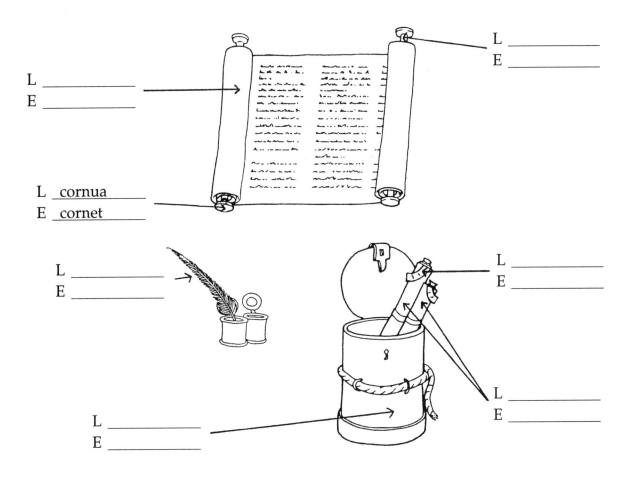

L _____
E _____

L _____
E _____

L cornua
E cornet

L _____
E _____

L _____
E _____

L _____
E _____

L _____
E _____

20.3 Plancus and the Sacred Crocodiles

Read the story below and then write the answers to the questions.

crocodīlī sacrī

There were many tourist attractions in Egypt, including the sacred crocodiles who lived near Crocodilopolis, Crocodile City.

Aristō cum uxōre fīliāque in adversum Nīlum nāvigābat. cum eīs ībat
Plancus, vir doctissimus, quī numquam tacēbat. ad urbem
Crocodilopolim iter faciēbant, ubi crocodīlōs sacrōs, bēstiās nōtissimās,
vīsitāre volēbant.

 in itinere amīcī templum antīquum Sōlis et pȳramidas vīdērunt. hae   *5*
rēs mīrābilēs omnēs dēlectāvērunt. Plancum valdē dēlectāvērunt, quod dē
monumentīs templīsque garrīre semper volēbat.

 tandem amīcī ad urbem Crocodilopolim pervēnērunt. ad lacum
contendērunt ubi sacerdōtēs crocodīlōs sacrōs cūrābant. hī sacerdōtēs,
postquam spectātōrēs in rīpā stantēs vīdērunt, "audīte vōs omnēs!"   *10*
clāmāvērunt. "nōlīte crocodīlīs appropinquāre! perīculōsum est
spectātōribus in extrēmā rīpā stāre."

Feeding time for the crocodiles.

sacerdōtēs crocodīlōs vocāvērunt. crocodīlī statim ad sacerdōtēs
spectātōrēsque natāvērunt. tum sacerdōtēs pānem et carnem et vīnum in
ōra crocodīlōrum posuērunt. postquam crocodīlī cibum cōnsūmpsērunt,   *15*
sacerdōtēs pannōs cēpērunt et dentēs eōrum lavāre coepērunt! spectātōrēs
fortitūdinem sacerdōtum laudābant. tum Plancus, quod crocodīlōs
propius vidēre volēbat, ad extrēmam rīpam prōcessit et dē vītā
crocodīlōrum garrīre coepit. subitō, prōcumbēns et garriēns, in lacum
inter crocodīlōs cecidit! omnēs commōtī mortem Plancī timēbant.   *20*
crocodīlī tamen ab eō celerrimē fūgērunt et Aristō Plancum ex aquā
trahere poterat.

 Galatēa, in aurem Helenae susurrāns, "crocodīlī" inquit "Plancum
audīre nōlunt. fēlīciōrēs sunt quam nōs, quī ab eō effugere nōn
possumus."   *25*

in adversum Nīlum	*up the Nile*
pȳramidas: pȳramis	*pyramid*
lacum: lacus	*lake*
in extrēmā rīpā	*on the edge of the river bank*
natāvērunt: natāre	*swim*
pānem: pānis	*bread*
carnem: carō	*meat*
ōra: ōs	*mouth*
pannōs: pannus	*cloth*
dentēs: dēns	*tooth*
propius	*at closer quarters*
commōtī: commōtus	*alarmed*
fēlīciōrēs: fēlīx	*lucky*

1 Which members of Aristo's family were with him?
2 How were they traveling?
3 What two things does the story tell you about Plancus' character?
4 What two sights did the friends see on their journey?
5 Why was Plancus particularly pleased?
6 What was special about the lake to which the friends hurried?
7 What were the spectators doing?
8 What warning did the priests give the spectators, and why?
9 What happened when the priests called the crocodiles?
10 What three things did the crocodiles have for dinner?
11 What did the priests do with the cloths?
12 How did the spectators react to what the priests did (with the cloths)?
13 What did Plancus do then, and why?
14 What happened to Plancus next?
15 How did everyone feel then, and why?
16 What was unexpected about the crocodiles' behavior?
17 Why do you think they behaved that way?
18 What finally happened to Plancus?
19 What was Galatea's explanation for the crocodiles' behavior?
20 In Galatea's opinion, who was luckier than she was, and why?

Present Participles

Complete the Latin sentences below by choosing suitable participial phrases from the box. Then translate the sentences.

> **participial phrases:**
> vīnum bibentēs   dē vītā dēspērāns   versūs sacrōs recitantēs

1   2

sacerdōtēs, _____ ,   mercātor, _____ ,
deae Īsidī sacrificābant.   in lectō recumbēbat.

3 hominēs, _____ , in tabernā sedēbant.

Complete the following by choosing suitable nominatives from the box. Then translate.

> **nominatives:**   iuvenis   fabrī   puellae

4 _____ , vitrum facientēs,   5 _____ , Barbillum quaerēns,
in officīnā labōrābant.   ad vīllam pervēnit.

6 _____ , rosās spargentēs, prō pompā currēbant.

Word Study

A *Match the Latin word on the right to the word which means approximately the same. Give the meanings of both words.*

1	effigiēs	a)	turba
2	ōlim	b)	poscere
3	postulāre	c)	et
4	appropinquāre	d)	quondam
5	agmen	e)	statua
6	cupere	f)	caedere
7	interficere	g)	velle
8	multitūdō	h)	pompa
9	-que	i)	adīre
10	ruere	j)	festīnāre

B *For each of the underlined words, give the Latin root. Then suggest a meaning for the underlined word based on your knowledge of the Latin root and its meaning.*

1 The <u>sermon</u> was more like a chat than a lecture.
2 There was a <u>duality</u> of purpose to his suggestion.
3 Uncle was an incurable <u>pessimist</u>.
4 Beethoven did not write that <u>sextet</u>.
5 After the storm, no one claimed the <u>derelict</u> ship.
6 Becoming a <u>quadragenarian</u> is a major event for some.

C *Based on the MEANINGS of the words in each group, pick the word which does not belong. Explain why it does not belong. Not ALL words have appeared on Checklists.*

1 unda aqua lūna lītus mare
2 domus templum dea āra sacerdōs
3 fundus urbs arātor horreum agricola
4 ursa arānea fēlēs aquila columba
5 ambulāre ruere contendere currere festīnāre
6 dīcere nārrāre nūntiāre dēspērāre respondēre
7 senex anus fīlia domina ōrnātrīx
8 nauta effigiēs faber prīnceps vīlicus
9 aula domus casa agmen aedificium
10 impetus mīles nauta faber sacerdōs

20.6 Euro-numbers

1 *Using the Latin numbers as a clue, identify the jumbled numbers of the other languages.*

	Latin	Italian	French	Spanish	Finnish	Romanian
1	ūnus	cinque	neuf	cuatro	kaksi	patru
2	duo	quattro	trois	seis	yksi	opt
3	trēs	sei	deux	nueve	kolme	şapte
4	quattuor	otto	dix	diez	neljä	unu
5	quīnque	uno	huit	tres	viisi	nouă
6	sex	dieci	un	dos	kuusi	cinci
7	septem	nove	quatre	siete	seitsemän	sase
8	octō	sette	six	uno	kahdeksan	doi
9	novem	tre	sept	cinco	yhdeksän	trei
10	decem	due	cinq	ocho	kymmenen	zece

2 *For which language is Latin no help? Can you think why?*

20.7 Medicine and Science

Read pages 176–180 in your textbook and answer the following:

1 What type of center did Alexandria become shortly after its founding?

2 What attracted scholars from all over the Greek world?

3 What were scholars eager to do there?

4 In what area did they make great strides?

5 What had Hippocrates already done for medicine?

6 How did he accomplish this feat?

7 Where and when did he live?

8 Because of his prolific work, what is he regarded as?

9 What do we still use of his today?

10 What was the Greek view of studying the body?

11 What was the Egyptian attitude toward the body?

12 Because of this attitude, why would scholars come to Alexandria?

13 Who was Herophilus?

14 What were his specialties?

15 What were two effective ancient remedies?

16 What were some unusual treatments for chilblains and toothache?

17 Describe the ancient procedure for tonsillectomies.

18 List at least six ancient procedures still practiced today.

19 What did Greek doctors insist on to reduce infection?

20 In what field did the Romans make vast improvements?

21 What did the Romans organize for their soldiers?

22 When were the standards set by Alexandrian doctors finally improved upon in western Europe?

23 For what other field was the Museum famous?

24 List the areas of study of Euclid and Eratosthenes.

25 Where was astronomy developed?

26 How did the Alexandrian scientists improve upon it?

27 What Alexandrian observation did Copernicus rediscover and when?

28 What did the Chaldeans develop and when?

29 What were their basic beliefs?

30 What two famous Alexandrian astronomers believed in the pseudo-science of the Chaldeans?

31 Describe three of Hero's engineering devices.

32 What were eight devices widely used in the Mediterranean world from the third century on?

33 For what three possible reasons did the Alexandrians and Romans not take advantage of their scientific discoveries?

Body Language

A *Using the following words, label the various parts of the body. Give an English derivative from each word.*

auris
capillī
caput
cervīx
dēns
lingua
manus
nāsus
oculus
pēs
tergum
umerus

B *The following Latin phrases contain "body words." Look up the meaning of these phrases. Explain their meaning; give an example of how they would be used today.*

1 arrēctīs auribus
2 manus manum lavat.
3 ex pede Herculem
4 mēns sāna in corpore sānō.
5 caput mundī
6 ā tergō
7 ā capite ad calcem.
8 corpus dēlictī
9 habeās corpus